2020: given the rapidity of change over the past 25 years, it feels as if we are living in a different world. An unforgivable exception is the racism still witnessed in America. The author lived through the Second World War, which created discipline throughout the nation. He was born into a loving family, and his elder sister remained close due to their shared experiences during 1939/45. He left school at eighteen and undertook his National Service. This proved a worthwhile challenge and, together with a commission, opened the way for an interview with The United Africa Company, very important within Unilever. He was 25 years resident in Africa, where he had a fulfilling career due to the support of the indigenous people. Could a young person find a similar challenge today?

To Daphne

The strength throughout my life

Alan Brownlow

Africa in the 20th Century

AUSTIN MACAULEY PUBLISHERS™

LONDON · CAMBRIDGE · NEW YORK · SHARJAH

All of the events in this memoir are true to the best of author's memory. The views expressed in this memoir are solely those of the author.

The author offers his apologies for the poor quality photographs, but they were taken using a 60-year-old camera and felt that they bring some authenticity to the story and era of 'Africa in the 20th Century'.

A CIP catalogue record for this title is available from the British Library.

ISBN 9781398430525 (Paperback)
ISBN 9781398430532 (ePub e-book)

www.austinmacauley.com

First Published 2021
Austin Macauley Publishers Ltd
1 Canada Square
Canary Wharf
London
E14 5AA

Foreword

This story is about my life in West and East Africa.

The year is now 2020 and changes have been so rapid over the past twenty-five years that one feels you are living in a completely different world. An unforgivable exception to this is racism as demonstrated by the events in America.

I lived through the Second World War, which gave you a sense of discipline. I was in a loving family with an elder sister who remained close probably due to the experience we shared during the 1939/45 hostilities. Leaving school at eighteen, I commenced my two years of national service, gaining a commission, and witnessed a number of my colleagues returning from Korea with life-changing injuries. It was during this period I was interviewed by The United Africa Company, at that time the largest company within Unilever. I left with the message: if you are still interested in a career in Africa, contact us when you have completed your national service. In September 1952 I joined UAC, at that time the largest company within Unilever. I spent six months in the London office working in various departments. After the March 1953 induction course, the eighteen attending would be posted to countries in Africa. Enquiring why it was The Gambia in my case, I was told it would give me the broadest experience of the company in the shortest time. This was probably correct and I arrived in The Gambia in April 1953. It should be remembered that although the Gold Coast was shortly to become an independent Ghana, all the other British territories were still part of the Empire.

I want to explain how I experienced Africa and how it reacted to my presence. I was fully conscious of what all European countries had gained from their empires, and this obviously changed over a number of centuries.

This story is an attempt to explain how Daphne, my wife, and I experienced extremely interesting, happy, and rewarding lives whilst being resident in Africa for twenty-five years. This was followed by ten years of frequent visits to assist those I had previously worked with.

I hope this manuscript will demonstrate that whatever I might have been able to contribute was only achieved through the support and in many cases dedication of African people.

I find it difficult to think that any young person could find a similar challenge today.

I refer in particular to those remote locations stationed many miles up the Gambia River. Every aspect of life depended upon your own decisions but on many occasions, you sought advice from the African staff. No telegraphic communication and certainly no internet.

Chapter 1 – The Gambia

I travelled from Heathrow airport, at that time consisting of huts with luggage weighed on an old platform scale. The BOAC aircraft was an Argonaut flying to Madrid, then Dakar, where one spent the night in a small room, rather like a cell. The next morning a short flight to The Gambia was accompanied by a small number of passengers.

The Gambia is the smallest country in Africa, thirteen degrees north of the equator. The river some 350 miles flows directly east from the Atlantic with narrow areas of land on either side. During the period October to March, it enjoys a very pleasant climate. This has sustained the economy in recent years as it has built a successful tourist industry. Shortly after acquiring this territory, Britain abolished the slave trade in 1807. Independence came in 1965.

Arriving at Yundum airport, a small old building with the runway consisting of metal mesh used during the second world war. I was greeted by smiling faces. First the customs officers and then the UAC driver who took me into Bathurst now Banjul, where I met the General Manager Tom Mallinson. A short and very pleasant man nearing the end of his career. As Chairman of UAC, he was a member of the Legislative Council headed by the then Governor Sir Percy

Wyn-Harris. Sir Percy was a member of the team to reach the highest point on mount Everest, prior to Sir Edmond Hillary.

A condition of service was that you were provided with furnished accommodation. You can imagine as the most junior member of staff, this was basic. I was met by a lady who together with her husband Bill Shepherd became very close friends. Meg was responsible for seeing housing was up to the required standard and settled me into my small flat. Meg also found me a reliable cook/steward and I was ready to spend my first night under a mosquito net.

I think sixteen expatriates were working for UAC, and in most cases, we established lifelong friendships. Sharing the same staircase to our units of accommodation were Murial and David Niven. Again two close friends and I suspect they probably gave me a meal that first night.

UAC in those early days would have been seen as a trading company, selling all forms of imported merchandise with a particular emphasis on textiles. It also had traditionally bought and exported produce, but with the advent of government marketing boards, this was no longer a major activity. However, in the Gambia, UAC had a special role in respect of the groundnut crop and it would not be an exaggeration to say the company was held in high esteem for the contribution it made to all sections of the community.

The business consisted of a motors agency with a servicing department. Kingsway Stores, the only modern retail unit. An insurance agency within the shipping department dealing with all import and export administration. There were a further six companies of comparable size operating at that time. These companies formed a platform for economic development but inevitable independence would change how the economy progressed.

As we now seek to establish a lost presence in these markets and enable our economy to thrive outside the European Union, we no longer have the likes of UAC. We are faced with numerous, relatively small, UK businesses all trying to establish their own distribution channels. I would also venture to say that the intervening years have awakened many nations to the importance of Africa.

Coming from the UK we were fortunate to enjoy a strong relationship built over many generations.

I cannot recall any apprehension as the people were all so friendly and welcoming. Crime as we know it today did not exist which enabled you to adopt a relaxed attitude to daily activity. Of the five main tribes, Mandinka and Fulani were the largest, with the majority being Muslim.

In 1953, I estimate the population would be in the region of 350,000. Now it is one of the most populated countries by land size on the continent of Africa, resulting from the oppressed peoples fleeing Mali and countries further east. I feel certain that the environment we were fortunate to have enjoyed will have changed beyond all recognition.

My arrival in April meant the groundnut season had ended, and the General Manager would shortly proceed on leave. His deputy John Mann, the produce manager, would move upstairs during the Mallinsons' absence. I was asked to keep John Mann's seat warm. All I seem to remember during this period was being faced with piles of paper all related to the groundnut season that had just ended. Occasionally there would be a few hides and skins to weight and value and that was about it until the next season began.

I was fortunate to get on well with John and his wife Isla and together with Angus McNicol we played many games of bridge. Bicycle number 66 was my transport for most of my time in The Gambia. This allowed me to reach the club where you could play tennis but I got very involved in cricket which had a high profile in Bathurst.

Over the intervening years, cricket has been overwhelmed by football, but in the '50s all former British protectorates had a strong cricket presence with strong interstate rivalry. The season was from October to March, so it was only my first season spent in Bathurst that I was able to get involved.

The next four were spent at river stations. I was probably introduced by Tim Laing. Born in Ghana where he had represented the country as a very useful batsman. He came to The Gambia as our chief accountant and played for his new country. When I met Tim, he had retired from the game but was a member of The Gambia cricket board.

During the period October 1953 to March 54, I would have played most weekends and although always seen as a bowler I did manage to make a few runs. It must have been the matting on concrete wickets. We played on the then very picturesque McCathy Square in the centre of Bathurst.

The time approached for the intercolonial match against Sierra Leone, scheduled over four days. Although I am sure it was not a public holiday, it was certainly treated as such. There were the receptions at the government house and Sir Percy Wyn-Harris spent time watching the match. We batted first and made over three hundred for seven before declaring. I was ten not out.

We took the field early on the second day and I had the good fortune to take crucial wickets in their early batting order from which they never seemed to recover. They followed on but failed to reach our first innings total. The Gambian public was thrilled and celebrations lasted for a number of days. Both sides had a balanced African/expatriate number. Bobby Madi, our captain, financed a county professional to coach each year. To me, this clearly demonstrated what the game of cricket has meant to so many of the countries where the British had a presence.

1954 Gambia versus Sierra Leone
Sir Percy Wyn-Harris seated centre

Moving back a little to my arrival when the weeks and months passed quickly in a period when there would be frequent rain.

I have to confess that in accepting a career with UAC, I knew that if all went well, Daphne would be able to join me after six months and we could be married. When attending her medical in Unilever House, by chance she met Mr and Mrs Mallinson.

On the 26th November Daphne was taken by my parents to London airport together with our wedding cake. This had been made by my godfather and Daphne found herself on the front pages of all the London evening papers standing at the bottom step of the aircraft, 'She takes the cake etc.'

All London evening papers
26th November 1953

Her flight route would be similar to mine, but she still had to overcome the night cell in Dakar. The Gambia next day, beautiful sunshine, and I remember having a message relayed by the pilot as Daphne made the flight from Dakar – 'Your Popsy is on board.'

An incident arose prior to Daphne's arrival which I think speaks volumes for the relaxed manner that so many

Gambians displayed. Daphne had sent a trunk in advance and I had to visit customs to clear the item. I probably was explaining the background when the first item the customs officer saw obviously belonged to a lady and the officer said, 'Close that immediately there are things in there you should not be seeing at this time.' He immediately released the trunk. These same worldly and warm attitudes were displayed on several occasions when we needed help. Taking our dog Tinker to the veterinary surgeon, Dawda Jawarra later became President of the country from 1970–94. I think this must speak volumes for these early days of independence. I can remember the odd political figure but not the dominant party. Here we have a quiet, professional, and unassuming man with a love of golf taking on the most important position in his country for a period of twenty-four years. I do not know what his political leanings might have been, but it would be true to say the country has never been the same since his departure.

Sir Dawda Jawarra
Prime Minister 1962–70
President 1970–94
Our friendly Vet in 1954

Daphne was staying with the Mallinsons on the night of her arrival, an attractive residence overlooking the Atlantic. They had plenty of experience in these matters as Daphne was the third bride following Muriel Niven and Emily Myers, making working in the Gambia so enjoyable. Of course, by this stage, I knew all those who would attend the wedding whereas Daphne with no relatives present was a complete stranger. I have always been amazed at the ease with which she adapted to a completely new environment so far from home. We were married by a Ghanian Father Lemere at St Mary's Cathedral Bathurst on the 28th November with a full choir making it a very special occasion. John and Isla kindly hosted a reception at their home in Fajara, A twenty-five-minute drive from Bathurst. Their home with views of the Atlantic has now been replaced by a large hotel.

Daphne 28/11/53
Arriving at St Marys
With Mr Mallinson

Daphne mixed easily with all present and soon became the best of friends to many during the months ahead. At about 7pm the General Manager's car took us back to Bathurst and of course, Daphne had no idea what to expect. I now occupied a larger unit overlooking the entrance to the river with the main road in front. I guess the building was well over a hundred years old and at that time there was a store below. Daphne took this all in her stride.

However, at about 10 pm there was the sound of heavy objects hitting the corrugated roof. This was colleagues returning from the reception. I think the shocks came the following morning when we discovered that Daphne's vail had been completely eaten by cockroaches. Then there were the rats running up the pipes in the bathroom as they returned from a visit to the rice store. I think we both accepted this was only a temporary phase of our new life and were fortunately compensated by all the positives.

Mrs Mallinson had taken a film of our wedding. It was a small Kodak film which you sent back to the UK for processing. This has resulted in us creating a library over sixty years. Daphne was responsible for this as she became a hairdresser for both male and female residents until she had made sufficient money to purchase our first cine camera. She made many lasting friends and together with her Kingsway credit account quickly settled to life.

Commencing the new groundnut season in October 1953, my task was to transit on behalf of The Gambia Marketing Board all the nuts coming into Bathurst by river sailing craft or lorry. There were two large stores each taking 2000 tons or more. The nuts in their shells were shovelled into bags if coming by the river, head carried to be weighted and the bags emptied on the cargo being created for the next shipment. The labour was organised and controlled by a headman, Sanjali Bojang. What a wonderful man he was, totally respected by those he employed. Strict but caring if the need arose. To me, he became a friend.

2000 tons Groundnuts

Ships having been loaded, there were probably ten shipments in a season.

I was advised that for the period September 1954 to April 55 we would go to Kaur. A small village just over 100 miles upriver with responsibility for the transit operation. Although by most standards the recently built house was brick and well mosquito proofed, you were totally on your own. There was no form of communication. Drinking water had been collected in tanks during the rainy season and all other water was rolled up in barrels from the river then pumped up to a feeder tank. A small generator had been installed, it never functioned and we used Tilly lamps or candles. Vegetables and meat could be purchased from the local market but most other essentials would have to be taken from Bathurst. I suppose as neither of us knew what faced us, we cannot recall any real apprehension. We were to make our overnight journey by a company launch, the Aduna. Having loaded all our worldly goods and supplies, I then went to The British Bank of West Africa. A sum of over £70,000 was collected to finance the UAC purchases of groundnuts. The money was in wooden boxes which held the appropriate number of sealed tins. There was a lockable cupboard on the Aduna. This is a significant sum of money by any standards. There was no security. Loaded into a vehicle driven to the wharf and onto the Aduna. Even if there had been a police presence in Bathurst, this was unlikely to be the case at Kaur. It really is another significant aspect of how today's world has changed. Memories are short but other than the apprehension mentioned above the cash just seemed another part of the task ahead.

We travel to Kaur
September 1954

So on a beautiful sunny day, we set off with our little dog Tinker.

The crews on both the company launches were very loyal and trustworthy members of UAC staff.

Kaur was some distance from the river but on arrival facing us were two narrow wooden wharves about 30 yards apart. From each, a laterite road ran inland some 300 yards. Between the roads was mainly water from the river. Below a hill stood our home for the next six months.

How they were aware of our arrival I do not know but on the wharf leading directly to our house were a group of smiling faces. Gambians I would rely upon each struggling with their simple lives. I will never forget Falamo the headman. He gave me so much support and advice during the two periods we were in Kaur. I can see him now in his long blue gown. Strangers, and they were going to carry this very large sum of money and our luggage up to the house. The office and strongroom were under the stairs leading to the living quarters. The strong room had brick walls with a very old door. I had a simple nine-inch key and prayed it would lock the door. From that time the key remained around my neck like a necklace and so we settled into a very new life. It was quite lonely for Daphne but she organised the large living area and things soon took shape. Her hobby was needlework and she would read extensively. Respected, she got on very well with local people and was never happier than when trying out her pidgin English.

For my part, there was a realisation of being completely on your own. There was no one to turn to for advice and in retrospect, I think this helped me in my future career. However, I come back to the fact that Falamo and his team were vital in all we did. My primary task was to transit the groundnut crop about 10,000 tonnes, on behalf of The Gambia Oilseeds Marketing Board. Then make five shipments over a period of six months. There was a marketing board clerk who also recorded the weights of deliveries.

My working week was to commence the transit operation from 8am to 12.30pm and break for lunch. Resume transit 1.30pm to 6pm During these hours there would be calls for other requirements such as cash for those buying on behalf of UAC. At around 6pm I would return to the house, take a bath where the water was the same colour when you got out as when you got in. Have a little liquid refreshment before the evening meal. Then complete all the office accounts and records for the day, probably finishing at 8pm and soon off to bed. This was my routine Monday to Saturday. Sunday morning it was downstairs to the office to prepare all records for the week including checking and balancing the cash account. I can still feel that cold shiver down my back when you opened the strongroom door. On very few occasions did things balance the first time. Finally, a large envelope was ready for a man who served us well over a number of years, to make the journey to Kuntour some 65 miles further up river. Kuntour had telegraphic communication with Bathurst and would relay our figures.

Our communication with the outside world was very dependent on a small battery radio able to pick up BBC Overseas Broadcasting. Very important to our lives in those days. Two river vessels were calling at Kaur on alternate weeks. The Lady Wright with a post office on board. It was said to be only one of two in the world at that time. The other operating on the Mississippi. A much older boat the Fuladu made trips on alternate weeks and both would deliver mail to Mr Carew a UAC trader in the village. Only a short distance, Mr Carew would send our mail to the house. We realised throughout our lives in Africa how much this meant to our family and we're both committed to writing each week.

In twenty-five years I cannot remember more than two incidents of this nature but will now recount the part my dear wife played in avoiding what could have been a very serious situation. She felt our provisions of rice was reducing rather quickly. Not unknown from those helping with domestic issues. However, when the person concerned went off to market, Daphne decided to have a look in his room. In doing so she moved his pillow and there was a nail file she recognised as her own together with a long key. The key was similar to the strongroom key I wore around my neck. She quickly replaced the pillow and contacted me. I sent an urgent message to the village policeman. Yes, the village had a policeman, and very efficient he proved to be. He made sure nothing had been disturbed and awaited our man's return. An arrest was made and a short court hearing found him guilty.

This in no way detracted from an important aspect of my assignment, loading a Scandinavian vessel with groundnuts bound for Europe. The vessels were small and could navigate up as far as Kuntour. They were involved in the wood pulp trade during the summer months in the Baltic. UAC profited from the vessel being loaded in one day. Normally arriving late afternoon it would anchor midstream and early the following day come alongside one of the small wooden wharves. This would normally be at the rear of the vessel. Eight very long palm rungs say 7 inches by 5 inches would be lashed together. On one side, small strips of wood nailed to the surface would assist the labour force in their climb. A picture will show what 2000 tons of ground nuts in their shells look like. At the base of the heap, you would probably have ten men with shovels.

They would each work with five carriers. Each carrier would receive one penny when the sack was full, as he made his way to the palm rung ladder. Having boarded, he poured the contents of his sack into the hold. Below was a team of men with shovels who moved the nuts to the centre of the vessel. Halfway through proceedings, the vessel would move to allow the front hold to be filled.

Loading shipment to Europe in one day

It is interesting to try and put into context what 1 penny per carrying would mean. Suffice to say that on these very rare days in their lives they could be earning a daily figure over half of mine. Considering that I would be earning twice the figure compared with a young man starting out in the UK, it clearly shows the distortions that have taken place in the intervening period. Labour consisted of those controlled by Falamo and there would always be an equal number coming up from Bathurst. If there was to be trouble this is where it came from. It is easy to imagine that when loading begins the ship is high in the water and this results in the palm rungs being at a very steep angle. These were the circumstances confronting me with industrial action for the first time in my life. The Bathurst labour refused to load unless they were paid 2 pence a bag. My reaction was to get a bag of nuts, carry it up the palm rungs and empty the contents into the hold. Amidst a great deal of laughter, the problem seemed to have been solved. The vessel sailed as they all did that season with the sun setting in the evening. The Captains varied but in the main made a welcome change to our lives.

Our second Christmas was a very quiet day for us personally but there was great merriment amongst the Gambian people and on Christmas afternoon they descended upon us. All very gaily dressed and with drummers beating away as they entertained us and themselves for two hours in the house compound. They were definitely not seeking any reward from us but feel sure we found a few sweets and biscuits. All very simple and a traditional pleasure.

We now entered a new year and there would be two changes to our lives.

The first was that Daphne would give birth to our first child in February, and circumstances would be very different from those experienced by most couples. Whilst I remained in Kaur, Daphne boarded the Lady Wright some ten days before the baby was due and was fortunate in being able to stay with Anne and Arthur Draper. They played such an important part in our lives and were wonderful people. At that time Arthur was the accountant and secretary to The Gambia Oilseeds Marketing Board. Totally dependable, with a keen sense of humour our friendship started in my early days when they lived opposite in a pleasant house overlooking the river.

This friendship deepened when Daphne arrived in the Gambia and met Anne frequently. They had no children of their own but treated the birth of our first child as if it was their own. So Daphne stayed with them, and I was totally unaware of any other information except the birth was due on 15th February. Anne was a retired nurse so that helped and although Daphne has never complained, it was a difficult time. The birth was in the new Bathurst hospital but with limited equipment. Doctors Mr and Mrs Derola were on hand but it was senior Gambian nurse Julie Williams who, over two days, delivered Katie safely on the 17th February. Daphne maintained contact with Julie up to the time she died.

Back to the Drapers home but there was only one thing on Daphne's mind. How do I get back to Kaur? There I was, oblivious to all that had happened. Engaged in the transit process when the Aduna arrives at the wharf and one of the crew came to me with a note from Ken Gibson which said, 'Alan could you come aboard I have something confidential to tell you.' I suppose there was a degree of apprehension as I went into the cabin. There was a glass of beer on the table and "congratulations, you are the father of a baby girl."

There were sixteen expatriates working for the company and because of my remoteness, I was the last to know I was a father. Ken was the merchandise manager for the middle river, probably eight years older than myself, a very good tennis player but I do not think any of us realised he was a Squadron Leader in bomber command and had come through numerous missions. With all the time we spent with Pat and himself, this only became known to us when we attended his funeral with a full RAF guard of honour present.

So back to Daphne and baby in Bathurst. The first avenue was to see if there were any ships available but the problem here seemed to be the ability to get on to the vessel with a baby. Then came Arthur to the rescue. The marketing board had a large comfortable launch, the Tia Senela. Two members of their staff visiting from the UK and wanting to go upriver Arthur arranged for Daphne and baby to travel with them.

Why they should want to go up Pakali Ba creek unless it was to shoot crocodiles is difficult to understand. This is exactly what they did and the very first picture of Katie is in Daphne's arms with the crocodile on the deck of the launch. Things have now changed in a positive way but at that time it was considered a sport. Having said that on many occasions when the fisherman had been out overnight there would be crocodile meat for sale and very popular with the local population.

Totally unaware of any of this I am sitting on the verandah at about 8 pm when on a very clear night I hear the engine of a launch. This would not be unusual but what I can never explain is why in this case I decided to go down the 300-yard road in the dark to meet that launch. God's gift. there was Daphne, my daughter, and all that they had brought with them. So in darkness with a lantern to help us, up to the house we went. I must admit I had made no prior arrangements for this wonderful surprise and as it was getting very much warmer we decided to sleep under a mosquito net on the veranda. The veranda itself was completely screened and seemed the best place to be. Katie was destined to spend the first few months of her life there. Everyone experiences the delight of their new baby but I cannot express the joy Katie has brought to my life. The only one of our three delightful children to be born in Africa she has always had an affinity for those with a connection to that continent. As with all things Daphne coped with every aspect of this different life and Katie did have early feeding problems. It was not until we returned to the UK that we were able to resolve this. I feel sure there would be many problems facing having a child in certain parts of Africa today and all I might say is that with modern communication things could be flown in. However, I am not sure you would find the unsophisticated loving atmosphere that surrounded us. The other major change was the Marketing Board's decision to build a decorticating plant in Kaur and it brought a Scottish couple to live nearby and this would change many things when we returned in October that year.

We travelled down to Bathurst in early April. Stayed with Anne and Arthur for two days before boarding MV Aureal. It was too large to come alongside so we boarded a small motor launch. We had a memorable day in Las Palmas before docking in Liverpool. As I had completed a twenty-five-month tour we were due five months leave. Other than to say the sun seemed to shine throughout this time the only thing I will mention having a connection with the company was, I had ordered a car through our motors department in the Gambia for export back to the country. Ten percent of the cost was required and this enabled us to be the proud owners of a two-tone silver and grey Vauxhall Crestor for the period of our leave. It was with us on our return voyage but quickly sold in the hope of stabilising our financial affairs.

The morning of our return was bright sunshine with quite a hard frost. We said farewell to our parents and the journey to Liverpool began. We remember stopping to see the lovely drive leading to Windsor Castle and with Katie in her cot on the back seat of the car we continued our journey. Into the hotel for one night and due to board MV Apapa the next morning. One problem I remember all too clearly was that we had failed to retrieve Katie's small pink potty from the car. Fortunately, I was able to reach the car. The Apapa was a much older ship but I recall a very pleasurable voyage to Bathurst. Strange that one evening we sat at a table with Geraldine Wright, wife of Tim who attended the same induction course as me. Our paths would cross again. We were not long in Bathurst and soon returned to Kaur where things had changed in quite a dramatic manner.

The Scottish couple had been there throughout and were joined by a Unilever engineer who had been living in the UAC house. Although requiring large quantities of beer, he was a pleasure to have to stay with us. It would not be long before the decorticating plant was ready to be commissioned. The area to stack the nuts in their shells remained the same. To the left was the plant with a frontage of 20m by 40m deep. There had been the major task of filling in the area between the two roads to make a storage area where the bags of decorticated nuts could be stacked.

So my routine for the second stay in Kaur was very much the same except when it came to loading the Scandinavian vessels. The bags of course were that much heavier and the loading price was doubled to 2pence per bag. There remained the problem that having got the bag to the deck of the ship it would have been a lengthy and chaotic process to use derricks to lower the bags into the hold. My solution was to have two palm rungs secured in a V shape with the grain of the wood facing into the hold. Down went the bags under the momentum of their own weight. Men in the hold would move the bags to their appropriate position. Those loading the ship were able to operate at the same pace as before and this resulted in all ships sailing within the same timescale. Otherwise, my routines remained the same but of course, we had the added joy of Katie.

I feel having to make most decisions on my own held me in good stead for the future. Almost throughout my career, I had the freedom to act on my own initiative and that made UAC such a unique company to work for.

Nothing would have been possible without the wonderful support of all the Gambian people I worked with in Kaur. They had no expectations other than to earn sufficient to maintain their simple but happy lives. As a community, they supported each other and my lasting memory will be of smiling faces and that special man, Falamo.

And so the launch came to take us back to Bathurst. We had the company cash, our limited belongings, and the key still around my neck.

We then spent our next six months in Bathurst returning to the same flat near the Drapers. I was now in the shipping department and became familiar with the administration involving both import and export. The company also had an insurance franchise. In both activities, there was well-trained Gambian staff and I cannot recall any major problem arising. We must still have had the car enabling us to get to the beach at Fajara. One trip nearly ended in disaster when we slipped off the muddy track and rested at a dangerous angle.

Fortunately, there were a number of Gambians nearby to help. Meeting friends again after the six months in Kaur was wonderful for Daphne and I was able to enjoy a few games of bridge and tennis. At an early stage, I had been advised my next assignment would be as the upper river merchandise manager stationed in Basse, 300 miles from Bathurst. Prior to leaving, I spent a period with the two merchandise departments in Bathurst.

Our home in Basse

Again into the unknown with a two-day trip by launch to reach Basse. We would have refuelled at Kuntour. Katie, now approaching two years of age, enjoyed the trip and Tinker was never any trouble.

Basse was very different. Gone were the mangrove lining both sides of the river and when you reached Basse in late September there were high banks to the river. The wharf and our house were on the south bank. The large company store with a small office overlooked the river. In the office was a strong room with the door having been left open. When leaving the previous year, the door had to be smothered in grease as during the height of the rains the strongroom would be underwater. This meant cleaning the door, hoping it would close and lock before taking a large amount of cash from the launch. The house was old, wooden, limited in space, on stilts in the hope that furnishings would survive the rains and any significant rise in the river. From the rear door, you went downstairs to a small room containing a Dover stove for all our cooking needs. Daphne soon got us settled in and Katie was able to spend time on the small veranda. After Kaur, Basse was like being in a metropolis.

There were other expatriates of differing nationalities, missionaries, and a small store with telegraphic facilities so that I could communicate with Bathurst or Kuntour. We formed a friendship with the district commissioner Philip Burkenshaw and his wife. A man dedicated to his responsibilities within the area. Respected by the senior Gambians he had regular meetings with. For all that may be said about colonial rule, I believe this was probably one of the most stable times for countries within the then British Empire.

Many indigenous African people would be unhappy to see this helpful and sympathetic period end. My role now was to maximise the sale of all items within the wide merchandise portfolio. To issue cash to those traders purchasing groundnuts and receiving surplus funds. There were selling price guidelines but for bulk purchases, there was obviously discretion. I shared a vehicle with my opposite number in Kuntour and at least every three weeks visited our traders to our north and south then over to the north bank where I remember in January/February the river was so low you could cross on foot. It was shortly after our arrival that the UAC tug pulling many barges with the merchandise ordered by traders whilst they had been in Bathurst. In my area, it had already been delivered to George Eid in Kossamar about 20 miles south. I received a message that there were a number of textile prints missing from his order. I immediately made my way to Kossamar to substantiate the position. Back to Basse and there was a similar message from George Banner 20 miles north. I quickly made my way to Fatoto finding the same problem. Making my way back to Basse, I contacted the police and on its return journey, the tug was held in Basse. Naturally, all the holds were empty but under the planks on the floors of the barges were the rolls of textiles. We were confident that the crew of the Tug, long-standing employees, were not involved. It was a small group of casual labourers who would have travelled on the barges. Arrests were made and punishment followed.

As I said, Basse was so different from the isolation of Kaur. The Roman Catholic priests were always at hand and Father Flinn became a regular visitor. It is only an observation but as a member of the Church of England, it seemed the Catholic Church was trying to lift local people in their ambitions for life and were prominent in the community. By contrast, the Anglican approach was to reach down to the ones they felt needed the most support. I would not suggest which approach was most needed but only say that all missionaries have played a vital part in the development of Africa and their legacy must be the tremendous growth of Christianity.

An interesting interlude during that season was to receive an invitation to join Prince Philip on the Britannia. He had been away six months and his last port of call was The Gambia.

The royal yacht came up and anchored off the government station at Mansa Konko. I travelled down by road and met up with Meg and Bill Shepherd coming from Kuntour. We went on board by launch and I remember shaking hands with Prince Philip at the top of the stairs. His comment being, 'I can tell you are with UAC from your tie.' At the reception, I was in a group enjoying a long discussion with Michael Parker, ADC to Prince Philip. An Australian and much of what he said was refreshing, but not sure it would be wise to commit some things he said to print. I persuaded Daphne not to come because of her pregnancy and she may not have forgiven me.

Royal Yacht

Daphne had spent most of this period healthy whilst expecting our second child. We always knew that Ian would be born in the UK. Daphne would once again be on her own and with Katie, they travelled downriver. Staying with Anne and Arthur before returning to the UK. I can well remember the day before they left walking with Katie along the banks of the river. At least being in Basse I could receive confirmation of their safe arrival at various destinations and would shortly be joining them in the UK.

We had made a reasonable contribution with sales volumes that season and it was time to close down the station, leaving the strongroom door well-greased and open. I returned to Bathurst and on to the UK.

This was the only birth when I would be with Daphne. So with three children all of whom one can be very proud of, her unflinching devotion has played a unique part in our lives. We returned from the UK and spent the next three months in Bathurst, I was the lower river merchandise manager.

We lived in a small brick-built house with a colourful garden. With Daphne being on her own while I was on tour this was an ideal location, especially as we had a small Duiker, commonly known as a Dik Dik, a small antelope. A particular friend for Katie but cannot remember how we came to acquire this delightful creature. Each week I was away for three nights and there were good rest houses to stay in. Obviously, our social life was greatly enhanced. In addition to the lower river responsibilities, at regular intervals, I had to make trips upriver visiting those traders who continued to operate during the rainy season, two trips I remember well.

Leaving Bathurst, one of the traders I had to visit was situated in the Pakali Ba creek. Yes, the same creek that Daphne had visited when she returned with Katie to Kaur. We reached our destination and the launch broke down. What could I do? Alhaji Betts was there, still under the spell of Bint el Sudan perfume. I held quite a large amount of cash and I asked Alhaji if I could take over his safe. No problem and he handed me the keys, but how could I return to Bathurst? Alhaji found a young man with a motorbike, who was prepared to undertake the journey. So leaving at about 6 pm and on very bad roads, we arrived at our destination at around 3 in the morning. The remarkable thing was I went up the stairs, turned the handle, the door was open with all occupants fast asleep. Where could you do that today? Again the young man who transported me could not have been more helpful. Not sure how much sleep I had but off to the motors workshop early next morning to explain the situation to Dave Gordon the engineer. The only UAC vessel available was the Gorse. Very old and slow, so we were back in Pakali Ba late afternoon but with sufficient time for Dave to complete repairs. I collected the cash, thanking all concerned, and continued my journey. On a subsequent trip, I was coming down the river with just one station to visit, Ballingho. It was dark and having had my supper decided I would get under the mosquito net and try to sleep. This proved impossible and about 10 pm I took the bicycle off the back of the launch and with a torch in hand made the two-mile journey to our traders' store. You can imagine his shock. Fortunately, he was a younger member of the team and with Tilly lamps I was able to check stock, watching the rats hide behind items on the shelves.

Finally, the cash was checked and I was back on the bicycle. I think the crew was pleased to get away from the mosquitoes and as dawn broke we were in Bathurst. I can always remember Duggie Bray at that time acting General Manager saying, 'Are you sure you called at every station.

When you think we were personally responsible for cash and any shortage was for your own account. Reflecting upon the conditions under which you were operating, it probably says we had a tremendous reliance upon the honesty of those we were dealing with. Fortunately, I did not experience a shortage.

So we come to our last six months in the Gambia, and for us, it was back to Basse. We arrived late afternoon with the two children and it was obviously a very busy time getting the cash off and into the strongroom. The house which had been unoccupied for six months needed cleaning, beds made, etc. It was necessary to ensure that fuel was available for the Dover stove. I imagine a rather tired family made their way to bed that night and I will always remember when a cup of tea had not arrived the following morning.

I made my way down the back stairs to investigate wearing my pyjama trousers and as I approached the kitchen I could see something was burning. Then an explosion and the realisation I had been burnt. The man in our employment Masana was standing outside the kitchen and he had obviously suffered from the incident. Daphne, hearing the explosion rushed downstairs in her nightclothes, returning immediately to bring a bottle of aqua flavour which she had purchased in Bathurst. I think that most of this found its way to Masana. Daphne, still in her nightclothes, ran into the village and it was not long before the new district commissioner Jeremy Howe arrived in his land rover. Very different from his predecessor but equally committed to his responsibilities.

Taking one look at me there seemed to be only one answer. Mattress into the back of the land rover and shortly the family were off to the nearest hospital, some fifty miles away at Bansang. How had this happened? Masana instead of collecting firewood the night before so that the Dover stove could be used had borrowed a primus stove from the launch.

Not knowing how to use it he had mixed the paraffin and methylated spirit. How fortunate one can be. Having made our way to Bansang, who should be there to greet us but Peter N'Dow, a young doctor I knew well in Bathurst. He was obviously very concerned when he saw the extent of the burns. Sent Daphne outside and began the process of peeling away all the burnt skin. I really cannot remember this, although conscious throughout. He did such a wonderful job that I have never had scars from quite a serious incident and will ever remain in debt to Peter.

When the family next saw me, I was covered in bandages and would be like that for a few weeks. I remained in hospital and Daphne made her way back to Basse with the key of the strongroom around her neck and now responsible for the company affairs in Basse. Well, it was not quite like that. News had made its way to Kuntour and almost as Daphne arrived, Bill Shepherd had made his way to Basse by road. No matter how much Daphne asked Bill to sleep on the veranda of the house, Bill being Bill, he insisted on sleeping upon the counter of the main store. I returned after a few days and funny in retrospect, everyone gave me a wide berth. I was still in bandages including my face and I think they thought I had leprosy. We had help from many quarters.

I recall an enjoyable Christmas with the children. There was a well outside the house, never used but at one stage there was the unusual sight of a snake at the bottom. One of the rare occasions we saw a snake during our years in Africa. The experience I now had given me confidence pertaining to my responsibilities and this made the stay in Basse, particularly with all the people who would call, a very pleasant period.

At the end of February, I received a message to close down Basse and move to Kuntour where I would remain, until we finally closed this main centre of operation in the river. Although we had stopped at Kuntour to refuel the launch, we did not know this location. At the height of a season, UAC would have four expatriates. Station manager, two involved in the transit of groundnuts, and a merchandise manager.

When we arrived, the last cargo had left for Europe and after I had taken over from the station manager, we were left with a pleasant young couple. Eric, we had met in Bathurst but at that stage, his wife Thelma was in the UK. They were both in Kuntour and Eric would assist me. We were fortunate to occupy a large duplex house with wide verandas and a brick-built office underneath. No rice or rats to bother one. Not knowing Kuntour there were new disciplines to learn and recall there were not sufficient hours in the day.

I can remember the General Manager, Mr Mallinson passing through by launch on his way to the upper river. I received a telegraph message from him asking for a lorry to be sent to Basse so that a quantity of rice could be transferred. I arranged for Jallow, our long-standing and dedicated employee, to take the lorry with Eric to Basse. About three days later, a very distressed Eric returned to Kuntour. When Thelma saw her husband, she collapsed and I carried her to my bed and assumed Daphne vacated hers for Eric. There had been a very serious incident.

Leaving Basse, Jallow had made his way down to Georgetown enabling them to take the ferry to the north bank of the river. He was the last vehicle on a loaded ferry. Eric had got out of the lorry and stood beside the vehicle. When it became Jallow's time to drive off, due to the weight of his load the front of the ferry tipped up, and despite his efforts, the lorry with Jallow and cargo slipped into the fast-flowing river. I immediately set off for Georgetown. Where the vehicle had entered the river, not at the deepest point, but very fast flowing and the vehicle had moved from the point of entry. Clearly demonstrating the spirit of the Gambian people, anyone who felt they could help was at the scene, prepared to work through the night. Secured by ropes around their waists, divers continued to search for the vehicle, and eventually, it was located. Help was at hand to bring the necessary hawsers for pulling the vehicle out, but securing was proving difficult. In the early hours of the morning, the task of retrieving Jallow and his beloved green Bedford began. The rice having drifted away eased the task. With Jallow in my vehicle, I will never forget the journey to the hospital where his post mortem would be carried out. A dedicated man who I am proud to call a friend in this life. Understandably I feel Eric and Thelma never recovered from this experience and the shadow seemed to be with us until it was time to leave for Bathurst. Being back to where we were married there was plenty to occupy us before departure for Nigeria.

Mid-April 1958 and with many lasting friends to share goodbyes with. None more so than Anne and Arthur Draper. We had experienced a very different five years than would confront most couples. I know we faced all the challenges together, but the Gambia and its people will always be a special part of life's journey. I hope we were able to give back a fraction of what was given to us. Daphne and the children would go to Lagos by the MV Apapa and they left a few days before me. Daphne met Mary Flintoff on that voyage and they have remained close friends. I was to fly with a night stop in

Accra, Gold Coast as it was in 1958. Imagine my horror when reaching Yundum airport the authorities waved me through with the comment, 'Do you realise your passport is out of date?'

It was five years and a few days since receiving my first passport in the UK. With a degree of concern, I boarded the plane. No problem in Accra, likewise in Lagos. The General Manager quickly got the document renewed. Not a good impression to commence a new stage of my career.

Chapter 2 – Northern Nigeria

It is an appropriate place and time for me to express a personal view of Empires.

I have already indicated that my experience of the relationship between the populations of British colonies in West Africa and our diplomatic service in the late 50s, was one of respect and appreciation, particularly amongst the older generations. Many said they did not want us to leave. However, this does not explain the exploitation that had occurred throughout the world in previous generations.

Whilst flying from Kano airport to the UK in the mid-fifties, aircraft were flying at lower altitudes and for many miles, it was possible to see the terrain below. Apart from the odd hamlet, mile after mile of nothing. Eventually, you approach the Mediterranean Sea and there is a fringe of buildings. Across the water and a completely different scene. Every European country had roads, rail, towns, villages, and farmland. Most European countries had an empire. This is not to suggest that populations did not work hard to improve their lives but what we must all accept is, where did the resources come from to make so much of this progress possible. In my opinion, we find it difficult to appreciate this fact because wealth gleaned, in many different ways and over centuries, flowed into the pockets of a relative few, including past royal dynasties.

On our way to Kano Northern Nigeria

Daphne and family duly arrived and for the short period we were in Lagos it was for me to meet those working for the company Gottschalck. A small German company that had been acquired by UAC. In 1958 it operated independently reporting directly to London. There were two main areas of business, building materials, and specialised textiles. At that time there was also a small office equipment section operating in Lagos. It gave us the opportunity of meeting old Gambia friends, Meg and Bill Shepherd, Muriel, and David. Niven, Margaret and Brian Hunt.

A section of staff
All making a contribution to the economy

Gottschalck Kano 1958

We were soon off to the airport in Ikeja, old and small in those days handling internal flights only. We boarded a DC3 to Kano with a stop in Jos, well known as the hill station, and ideal to take a relaxing break. The stop was brief but that flight remains in my memory because it was one of those rare occasions I flew with the children who made the journey as if it were a regular experience.

Kano airport handled all international flights and was impressive particularly by comparison with Heathrow at that time. There to meet us were Geraldine and Tim Wright. Tim and I had been on the same induction course. Geraldine, you may remember we met on the Apapa. They could not have been more helpful during the handover period. They lived in a very pleasant bungalow in Nasarawa a short distance from the centre of Kano. During the handover period, we would live in a very large and comfortable apartment above the company showroom. I was soon to learn that most aspects of the business were very different from the Gambia. The accounting returns were on a very large sheet of paper and when complete for sending to Lagos I was never sure I really understood all the details.

However, once Tim left I was again on my own.

It's difficult to describe Tim, who I liked immensely. I think he was always a risk-taker and without a doubt a practical joker as was evidenced in the future. However, they made us very welcome.

Two things I will never forget is the journey to Katsina, a small station about 100 miles from Kano. The speed Tim drove there and back on not very good roads was an experience I would not wish to repeat. In the last week before they left, Tim and Geraldine insisted they should take us to the open-air cinema situated on the road to the airport. Who in today's world would consider going out and leaving two small children in the hands of a domestic employee we hardly knew. We gave in to the pressure and off we went. Sitting, whilst the advertisements were playing, a message came up on the screen, 'Would Mr Right come to the reception?' I turned to Tim and said, 'Do you think that they may be referring to you?' Tim duly went and found that Usman had phoned and asked that we return as Ian was crying. Usman was with us for many years and became almost part of the family until the Biafa war when he joined the Nigerian air force.

So to my new responsibilities. I had a staff of about twenty-five spread over sales, clerical, storekeepers, labour, and night watchmen. I was there to obviously maximise sales but a daily routine was to check cash and on a monthly basis, a stock check was required. I had an engaging assistant manager John Lashado. Not quite sure which part of the country he came from but with northern origins he had no involvement with the Kano police. John was always someone you could turn to for sound advice. At the height of the season November to February, an expatriate with special knowledge of the textile trade would be with us. I think we all quickly settled into this new life and most things were available in Kano. At that time Kano was typical of main centres in Nigeria where you had three UAC companies operating but reporting separately to the UK. By far the largest was UAC Nigeria with all departments reporting to their general manager in Niger House Kano. During my period there the post was held by Gordon Wilson, a very capable man destined to become Chairman in Lagos. Gordon always included Daphne and me in their Christmas party and the very enjoyable gatherings they were. Almost as large was G B Ollivant who reported to a head office in Manchester. Interesting that the manager responsible for their part of the business that I might well have considered a competitor was Jim Louden. Jim was captain of a very good Kano cricket team and I enjoyed being a member of that side.

My staff was from all parts of the country with a limited number from the northern region. I think possibly two in textile sales with others being night watchmen and labour. A few more from the west but the majority came from eastern Nigeria. The clerical staff was Ibo, led by a very quiet, reserved but extremely efficient man. It was he who enabled me to get to grips with these new very large accounting documents. I always felt there was cooperation and harmony in the team. I will return to this ethnic situation later.

The north in those days felt regal. The Sardauna of Sokoto could almost be King and indeed all the Emirs were very special people within their community.

Sir Ahmadu Bello KBE. 1910 to 1966 was the only premier of Northern Nigeria and Sir Abubakar Tafawa Balewa, a prominent figure in the north at that time was later to become the first prime minister of an independent Nigeria.

Fridays of course were prayer days for most people. One never experienced hostility and people went about their daily tasks. The city was clean and the many homes small but cared for. At no time did we witness any form of starvation and this was also our impression on the many occasions we travelled extensively in the North.

Up to 1928 Northern Niger had been governed by The Royal Niger Company. In that year Lord Leverhulme acquired the Niger Company and together with the African and Eastern Trading Company, UAC was established.

Back to the day job where I was still on a learning curve and no doubt there were not enough hours in the day. This was particularly the case in 1959 when the country announced there would be an international trade fair as part of the festival of Kano. Leslie Coppard who had taken over as General Manager was very keen that we participate and he supported me in many ways. A large area was set aside by the Kano administration and one applied for a specific plot. With the range of products we held, I realised we needed a reasonably sized stand and from memory, I think it had an open frontage of 150 metres by 70 deep. A lady responsible for the display in Lagos came up and did a wonderful job of the textiles display. This was on the left as you approached the stand. All other products in building material together with office equipment occupied the rest of the space. This was apart from the bathroom suite with running water. Although I say it myself, amongst local people it was probably the highlight of the exhibition. I will talk quite frequently about wind pumps and that we held the Climax franchise. Outside the stand and central we had sunk a tank of water and erected the windpump above. Not only could you see the sails of the pump as you entered the exhibition when you entered the stand there was water flowing through the taps of the bath and washbasin. It was a challenge at the time but enjoyable in retrospect. We established a strong friendship with the Woods family in Sokoto. I never knew his Christian name, all referred to him as Timber. He was responsible for the water supply in that area and during the period we were in Kano a number of windpumps were purchased. We visited Sokoto as their guests and on one occasion witnessed a very impressive Durbar. I can remember a BBC team driving alongside the horseman as they raced to the end of the field. We were all in ties and jackets, ladies with hats and smart dresses. This with all the colourful national dress created an atmosphere and importance of the occasion. I come back to the fact that this could have been a royal event. I cannot imagine the same feeling in the southern parts of Nigeria. Kaduna was the capital of the north. Our good friend Eric Fry from Gambia days was the district manager.

Festival of Kano 1959

Gottschalck Festival Stand

Moving forward a few years to make the point that in my opinion, Kaduna was the location the Biafra war started. I feel very strongly that the balance of our staff in Kano with a preponderance of very good Ibo staff was at the heart of this problem. One indigenous community trying to address the imbalance as has been the case in many parts of Africa. One usually looks back with positive memories and this must be the case in respect of Kano. Katie and Ian seemed to thrive, Daphne as usual made a number of friends and it was a good posting for my introduction to a new part of the business.

I never quite took to the harmattan winds and dry conditions of the north, preferring the more humid south.

Early in 1959, I received a letter informing me I should proceed on leave and upon my return, I would be posted to Aba in Eastern Nigeria.

Chapter 3 – Eastern Nigeria

Stephen, our third child, was born early in July. Rightly or possibly wrongly I did not protest when informed I should be in Aba by early June. This meant of course Daphne would once again give birth on her own to one of our children. On the one positive side, I could establish our new home. An identical bungalow to Kano with one air conditioning unit in the main bedroom. Without the authority to install an additional unit for Katie and Ian, my answer was a relatively small hole in the wall between the two bedrooms. It seemed to work.

Now to imagine Daphne's journey. Stephen was about six weeks old and my father would have taken them to Heathrow. No M25 in those days and I always remember it as quite a long journey with many narrow roads. I think it was either a Britannia or the American Stratocruiser flying into Lagos. That would have been a seven-hour flight with the three small children. It would have been a difficult task clearing all the formalities in Lagos. In my experience, Nigerians were always helpful in these situations and probably were continuously talking to Katie and Ian. Daphne's major problems arose when informed her onward flight a DC3 she was weight listed. The times she has said how distressing this occasion had been for her and it has always raised a smile when she threatened walking to Port Harcourt. Her pleadings paid off as she got on this small aircraft and finally arrived. Aba about 40 miles north of Port Harcourt, roads not the best, and although the car was air-conditioned they would all be feeling the heat.

And so to life in Aba, one of the happiest stations of many we served in Africa. Funny after all these years and with no disrespect, my description of Aba would be 'One Eyed'. There were no outstanding features unless you considered the relatively new brewery. A vast community of vibrant people representing one of the largest trading centres in Nigeria. Having spent the period in Kano, I was familiar with how a branch functioned and this made me more relaxed with my responsibilities.

Aba was different in its reliance on specific areas of the textiles trade. Building materials also tended to be aligned to the market trader which certainly placed pressure on margins. Office equipment rather like Kano, available to someone wanting a typewriter or duplicator. Again an excellent staff with most coming from the Eastern region. An exception was a very able assistant manager from the West. The business progressed and I do not think there was a concern about reaching targets. Aba was unique as a previous manager had engaged an artist. Certain Dutch wax prints could demand a very high premium and Gottschalck was fortunate in having a variety of prints, a leading print designed by the Aba artist. What will always remain in my memory, is the only occasion when I was asked for money to secure an order. A British man working for public works came in with a large order for cement. Needless to say, there was no transaction.

Aba club was the centre of all social activities and was well supported with individuals taking responsibility for events. I played cricket and there were matches in Port Harcourt and Onitsha. Dr B.J Ikpeme was our captain. Nearing the end of his career, a wonderful gentleman and deeply involved with the Nigerian cricket association, having represented his country. I played my last game of rugby, but tennis featured highly during that period. Daphne was outstanding on the drama front, taking the leading role in a number of productions. This took her back to her younger days when she had so much enjoyment in various productions.

I must now introduce two great friends and I expect we first met at the club. Ad and Frouka Verhoven from Holland, Ad, who was one of the brewing team at Nigerian Breweries, was larger than life both physically and in character, but Frouka could hold her own. Both so kind and always prepared to help others.

At home, the children all seemed happy and gradually met others of the same age. We were faced with having Stephen christened as were a Scottish couple living near to us. Arrangements were made to have the two boys christened at the leper colony in Itu some fifty miles north of Aba. Ad and Frouke were Stephen's godparents and we all travelled up in convoy on the appropriate Sunday. The colony consisted of two long buildings with palm leaf roofs, situated near a river. There was this feeling of being in an environment that experiences so much sadness and yet there was a reverential calmness. The short service over, it was time to make our way back to Aba. The little boy christened with Stephen died shortly after. A moment of deep reflection.

Although there was a river in Aba where many swam, I did not think this was suitable for the young children. When in Sokoto, I had seen and experienced the small swimming pool our friend Timber Woods had constructed and decided it would be ideal for our family. In front of the bungalow and in a reasonable time, with no doubt Katie and Ian thinking they could assist, the square pool was finished. Now came the difficult part. I finally had to lay a small pipe over about twenty metres of the garden to obtain a water supply. However, the finished article seemed to give a great deal of pleasure to both small and large. It was a salutary feeling to see bullet holes in the sides of the pool when visiting this area after the war.

The children had a great time particularly at Christmas when the club arranged a special fancy dress party. I think this was the time of a cricket match when ladies dressed as men and the latter as ladies. The district commissioner played a major part in making this occasion such a success. I played bridge with the Verhovens and a colleague. Very much the case when Daphne was at her drama rehearsals. We did have one very bad week when both Daphne and I were in bed with dengue fever. The UAC doctor came up from Port Harcourt but that week must have demonstrated how good our Nigerian staff was.

Then the new general manager for Gottschalck, Peter Tueart, and his wife Eileen came on tour and had an evening meal with us. Always difficult first meetings but it seemed to go well with Daphne and Eileen forming a friendship that would develop in the future. Shortly after this visit, I received a letter from Peter saying I should be prepared to move to Lagos as I was to head up the office equipment department.

In a relatively short period, I had experienced Northern and Eastern Nigeria and now moving to the West and the then capital city, Lagos.

Chapter 4 – Western Nigeria and Lagos

At this point, I wish to say how I saw the political profile of the country and believe it remained this way until well after independence. It was not a case of numerous tribes trying to have their voices heard. You had a stable situation where the Hausa voice represented the North with the Sardauna of Sokoto and Tafawa Balewa as leaders. In the East it was the voice of the Ibos led by Nnamdi Azikiwe. In the West, the Yoruba voice, led by Chief Awolowo. Problems of the future came from within these groupings.

Within the Gottschalck business, there had long been management responsible on a Nigeria-wide basis for textiles and building materials. The office equipment seemed to have been concentrated in Lagos with branch management having the only influence outside the capital. Little did I appreciate that I was on a long journey, possibly unique within UAC, but I had been given the opportunity to build a business within the country. This was only going to be achieved through the dedication and training of Nigerians. I would never in any way be technically competent but realised from the start that my responsibility was to plan and guide the future.

There were two stages to this part of my career, the former about three years with Gottschalck reporting to London, followed by the amalgamation of the Gottschalck and GB Ollivant interests to form a Business Equipment Division reporting to Manchester. I will mention two things concerning the former stage. Firstly, under Gottschalck a service training school had been established and this was managed by a former typewriter mechanic Felix Osifo. I will follow his career and we remain the best of friends.

It was clear, the business was top-heavy with expatriates. In some ways understandable due to the nature of the business, but not sustainable. I found the same situation existed within G B Ollivant.

I was asked to fly to the UK and Manchester with Albert Memmott, a UAC main board director for whom I had the greatest respect. I know Albert would have preferred to keep the business in London. I must say that being part of an organisation where the emphasis was trading in consumer products, did raise problems over the years.

I was introduced to the management team in Manchester with David Wolff being the main point of contact. David was in the latter days of his career, but we respected each other and the direction I decided to take was rarely questioned. Here I was just ten years into my career, being invited to manage a small business with so much growth potential. This would only be accomplished by a well-trained team of Nigerians in conjunction, at differing times, by the presence of expatriate specialists.

Back to Lagos and the task of rationalising property, products, and staff. The showrooms were opposite each other in Broad street. This enabled us to use the Ollivant premises as our main showroom with offices above. The whole of the Gottschalck building with the workshop behind became the main service centre and was to play a vital part in our future progress. When it came to products, we were spoilt for choice and we finally represented Imperial as opposed to Royal. Gestetner rather than Roneo and so on. Computers were some way off and we had excellent products across the complete range. Obviously, the question of expatriate personnel and their individual contracts had to be thought through sympathetically.

I do not think that any Nigerian staff on either side were reduced other than by natural wastage. Most Nigerians were anxious to learn thus enabling them to advance. We used the Lintas agency to formulate a new image for the business and we finally agreed upon Business Equipment and Methods. BEAM was born. The methods represented the loose-leaf accounting and other systems designed by Kalamzoo. Service would always remain a separate unit with the objective of quickly improving the standard and accessibility of service over the extensive range of equipment. Shortly after I appointed Felix Osifo as service manager. Various service specialists from the agencies we represented came to the training school and this enabled us to widen service facilitates outside Lagos.

BEAM STAND

Four diverse product groups were formed. The first was Gestetner, which handled the duplicators, offset printing machines, and office supplies; a Nigerian, Gabriel Adebanwe was the manager, but over long periods we had a senior Gestetner employee stationed in Lagos. The second group, Machines and Supplies, produced a number of different Imperial Typewriters, Franking machines, and Sweda cash registers. The third group was Furniture and Security, which produced Sankey Sheldon steel furniture and Chubb security systems ranging from central bank strongroom doors to everyday wall safes. The final group produced Kalamazoo Accounting Systems. These machines were early evolutions of the original computers and would record data by punching holes into long pieces of card.

There was a large depot in Apapa and branches in main locations throughout the country.

The importation of goods was affected by Nigerian Independence in 1960 and one would see many more changes over the years that followed.

Gradually we had management in Kaduna, Port Harcourt, and senior staff in Benin and Ibadan. Apart from Kaduna initially, these were Nigerian members of staff. The range of service coverage in all locations widened to include Sokoto, Maiduguri, Calabar, and Warri. Over twelve years profitability increased significantly. At an early stage of development, being in the field of capital equipment I introduced commission on sales. However, you soon learnt how careful one needed to be in avoiding potential distortions, thus undermining the whole process.

The growth in Lagos was such that we needed additional space. I have to thank a GBO director at that time and now a dear friend who assisted in our taking over most of what had been the entire HQ of Gottschalck. The two upper floors were completely changed to our needs with my office facing Broad street. As the years passed and imports became restricted and the country understandably wished to encourage local manufacture, we made some early and what proved to be profitable changes. Metal Furniture Nigeria Ltd owned by a gentleman I came to know and respect, manufactured an assortment of metal items. Manchester office negotiated an arrangement with Harvey, who was in the office metal furniture field, to hire an engineer with designs for the complete range of steel furniture to Metal Furniture Nigeria Ltd. They Manufactured Exclusively under the name of Beam Steel. Subsequently, we made arrangements with Harmony House to produce under our name a very attractive range of wooden desks.

We had for some time assembled Typewriters from imported parts and other equipment was to follow.

Kalamazoo had a particular problem having been designed locally, accounting systems etc. had to be sent back to the UK for printing. We decided to establish our own printing press in Apapa. The success of this was due to the dedication of a Nigerian, Morgan Soares. It was always impressive to see this department in operation.

In 1968 I was asked if I would go to East Africa for three months. Based in Nairobi but also to see if looking to the future, the office equipment business in Tanzania and Uganda were viable.

In many ways, Kenya was a shock. Whereas in West Africa there were generations of English spoken, in Kenya it seemed we were almost in the first generation. In many ways, over the years people from the Asian continent occupied positions from senior clerk to junior manager. Different but with similarities to the Ibo situation I found in Kano. This would lead to unrest in the future. Totally unacceptable in the manner it happened, but what Amin did to reduce the Asian presence in Uganda was an example. In many ways, the countries differed and this was reflected in the leaders at that time. However, it soon became clear that it would be difficult to establish a worthwhile office equipment business. Towards the end of my stay with Beam, we inherited the Burroughs Accounting Machine agency. They had just moved into the punch card process which would lead us into the computer age. It was always likely to be a struggle due to the number of expatriates required. However, what it did give me was the opportunity to appoint Bob Perone service manager, and to move Felix Osifo across to head the Machines and Supplies

Department. I spoke earlier about Felix Osifo. Over my years he went to the UK for training and development on many occasions including Henley business school. After some time he told me he nearly resigned as he thought he was being demoted when moved from Service Manager. Later in 1975 when I was asked to take up another appointment, on my recommendation he succeeded me as General Manager. Later in his career, he was appointed to the Board of UAC Nigeria. A very religious and self-made man, it has been a privilege to be a friend and we still correspond and meet when he is in the UK.

It was pleasing to see in 1979–80 results, well after I had left the portfolio of GBO business showed Beam Nigeria was the most profitable operation with a working capital well below others.

Our Lives in Lagos Nigeria

Lagos in the early 1960s was congested in respect of traffic numbers, but manageable, certainly if you were on the Island. Then as the amount of traffic increased, the government introduced the last number of the registration plate should be odd or even. Numbers applied to alternate days so two cars were required. I think this was my only brush with the law. Having the wrong number I had to take the car to a special holding area. The punishment, a rather long walk. Then on the occasion we went to Takwa on Saturday driving in the left-hand lane returning on Sunday we were faced with driving in the right-hand lane. We lived in Ikoyi where over the years we had three different houses, all comfortable with pleasant gardens. Victoria beach and the sea were easy to access and as mentioned the climatic conditions suited us compared with the north. All those we personally employed served us well with little supervision. There were major changes over the years caused by the political situation in the country. It may have been because I never seemed to master their real names, they were Little John from Kano days. Corporal who had seen military service and Wednesday, actual name Nwanzi. As the years went by they became almost part of the family and always looked forward to the children being in the country. I can remember Wednesday mixing the Yorkshire pudding on a Sunday and still follow his method with success. So both in the office and at home, we were in a very cordial atmosphere. I think it would be true to say that in those early years both Nigerians and expatriates were more likely to relax on their own.

We had a small motorboat and were able to launch in a stretch of water near the house.

Then off up the creeks or Tarkwa bay, both were a sheer joy. Shortly after coming to Lagos, British rule came to an end. Sir James Robertson relinquished his position as Governor-General in 1963. My impression is that he was highly respected and Daphne had the pleasure of meeting him at the Lagos Trade Fair. As touched upon previously, there has been an impression that numerous different tribes were manoeuvring for power. Throughout my years there was never a change with the North represented by the Hausa. East by Ibo and West Yoruba. It certainly seemed at the time of independence there was a stable relationship and the North accepted Nnamdi Azkiwe as the President of the First Republic. Sir Abubakar Tafawa Balewa from Bauchi in the North continuing as Prime Minister. The West was well represented in the new parliament. Things seemed to be moving along well and we were certainly unaware when we left Ikoyi early in January 1966 to drive to the airport with children returning to school. As we approached the marina we passed the house of the Prime Minister who had been killed that night, as had the finance minister who lived a short distance further on. It was only when reaching the airport we actually felt a military presence. All those flying to London then faced a major problem as the VC10 aircraft had been taken by the military and flown to Kano. Not sure when it returned but we cleared formalities and irrespective of the circumstances we were allowed to accompany the family to the departure lounge. Not sure where you could have found such a sympathetic attitude. There was no question of expecting recompense on the part of officials. Then we were faced with a long wait.

Quite a surprise to all when at about 3 pm a French aircraft arrived and all passengers could be flown to Paris. We were pleased but somewhat apprehensive when Katie and Ian departed. They seemed to take it all in their stride and eventually reached their destination. For us, it was a different situation. We were not allowed to return to Ikoyi and this would last at least two days. Friends to the rescue.

Meg and Bill Shepherd were residents in Ikeja at that time and sheltered us for the two days. I can remember the provisions being hastily purchased from the local Kingsway. Making our way back to Ikoyi there was a heavy military presence but no undue delay. We had been away for three days but the house was in its usual tidy state confirming the loyalty we enjoyed. However, there were changes as the Ibo gardener decided he should return to the East and this was a familiar trend that gathered pace as years unfolded.

Lagos Trade Exhibition
Daphne with Sir James Robertson

I am not familiar with all the details surrounding the very dangerous situation that occurred in Kaduna, with a large loss of life. A major Chuwuma Neogwuz led a coup d'état in 1966 which overthrew Azikiwe and his government. In January, General Ironsi became President of the second republic, but this lasted only till July 1966 when he was assassinated and the third republic headed by General Yakubu Gowen came to power.

During the period up to the Biafian war, there were tensions but most things functioned. There had always been strains on the infrastructure, in particular electricity supply. Lagos had an excellent club with an attractive golf course, more of which I will mention later. Good meals were available in many parts of Lagos. We always felt the Chinese food at the Cathy Restaurant in Lagos was the best we have tasted. The Bagatelle club, always very popular. The lad on duty would close the door of the lift and race you to the top floor. Welcoming you with an open door and of course, this was a way of earning a little extra money. So there was plenty to enjoy amid mixed communities. But of course, it was the sea, sunshine and the opportunity to play any sport. Football was gathering larger numbers as the national team emerged. Rugby was played but unfortunately, cricket seemed to have lost ground. Tennis is what I turned to especially when Ad Verhoven returned to the Lagos brewery.

In both houses we occupied in Ikoyi there were badminton courts in the garden. This provided tremendous enjoyment, particularly when the children were out on school holidays. Daphne always took a great interest in the gardens where with a healthy rainy season plants grew well. Also a large aviary with a wide selection of colourful birds. The only problem was when the gardener found a small snake under their drinking bowl. This with our delightful little dog Susie and a talkative African grey parrot meant there was plenty to occupy Daphne. We did have a television but it was never an important part of our lives.

The company had two chalets at Tarkwa and during school holidays Daphne and a close friend would take the children to stay for periods of up to five days. Never a problem, demonstrating how safe we all felt. I toured our branches on a regular basis and can remember the first occasion Katie was flying out on her own, aged eight. I arranged my journey back to Lagos on her flight. Then later when Daphne and I toured the whole of the north by road. Ibadan then north to Kaduna, Zaria, Sokoto where Daphne always remembers the strong smell of Bint el Sudan. East to Kano, Maidugeri, Jos, back to Ibadan and Lagos. I suspect approaching 2000 miles.

Unfortunately, it resulted in my being in bed with jaundice. Daphne always had a keen interest in local traditions and took every opportunity to speak with local residents, an important point I wish to make and I will exclude conditions that must have pertained in Eastern Nigeria during the war. In all our travels we never witnessed the poverty and tragic scenes we continually see throughout the world today. Small settlements growing their own food and contented with a simple life. There were schools and the majority of children would have access to education.

And so to the 3rd Republic with President Gowon taking office on 1st August 1966 at age 32. I believe that his rank was Colonel at the time. The first thing I will always remember is that very young face on television saying, 'To keep Nigeria one is a job that must be done,' and he did. My impressions were always of a compassionate man, determined that it was in Nigeria's best interest to remain united and to that end, he worked tirelessly and against many obstacles. Africa has a number of great men of the twentieth century and from what I observed his name should rank along with those of Nelson Mandela and Bishop Tutu in making what has been a great difference to the lives of its peoples.

Nigeria is one of the leading nations on this important continent and I do not feel that the same leadership apart from his colleague Muhammadu Buhari has to lead the nation since he was deposed whilst attending a meeting of heads of state in Kampala.

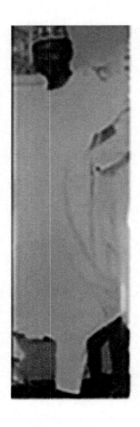

General Yakubu Gowon

In Lagos, things went on very much as normal even when the Biafrian war began in 1967. One enemy aircraft did fly to the capital but we were not aware of this. We could in various ways communicate with our colleagues in the East, but their supplies of stock were almost impossible. I think it was 1968 and I was due to proceed on leave, but before doing so I, with colleagues Stuart Brown and Brian Holland, drove to the Midwest to visit branches in Benin and Warri. Brian Holland had arranged to meet up with his Kalamazoo supervisor on the west bank of the Niger to give him a number of orders designed and printed in Lagos. Stuart Brown and I visited Warri and the branch in Benin. We retired to the UAC rest house and Brian duly arrived later. We were awoken in the early hours of the next morning by gunfire. It was a little time before we realised that shells were being fired at the residence of the Mid-West Governor Brigadier Ejoor. From the centre of Benin, the UAC bungalow was in direct line with the Governor's residence. We spent some five hours in the corridor, on the floor, praying we would not receive a stray shell. In the afternoon all seemed quiet and that was because the Biafran troops had driven on to establish a bridgehead within a reasonable distance from Ibadan. Obviously, there had been little resistance to this attack.

We have to thank the British consulate who quickly organised a convoy to Sapele. This would enable those wishing to return to Lagos to travel on the last cargo vessel bound for Lagos. The UAC plywood factory and plantations in Sapele were closing and I can remember whilst waiting to board the vessel helping check and secure the numerous properties. I should mention that at no stage were the limited number of Biafan soldiers any problem. We boarded the vessel on a sunny hot afternoon and it was a matter of finding a reasonable spot to spend that day and night. We choose the top of a covered hatch behind the bridge structure.

The voyage down the narrow river with thick forest on either side was absolutely breath-taking. At times it was forwards and backward to get around small bends in the river. Dark but dry when we finally reached the open sea and suddenly that gust of cool air. The temperature decreased as the night progressed and the only real problem was that someone on the opposite slant of the hatch had a dog. Every occasion it wanted to spend a penny, it came to the apex of the hatch. We arrived in Apapa nearing midday and within forty-eight hours I was on a flight to the UK.

Throughout the twentieth century, oil and its availability have been a desire of most nations. Nigeria had enjoyed large deposits, particularly offshore. There is no doubt this has changed nations and not always for the better. The way wealth is distributed and the potential corruption it can cause. This I regret was very much the case in Nigeria, when contented lives quickly became dedicated to how much personal wealth could be accrued. The many who went about their devoted duty know who they are and can hold their heads high. Unfortunately, it changed attitudes within this great country and in the eyes of the outside world.

The Tuearts became good friends and after being my General Manager we enjoyed many evenings of bridge. I played with Ad Verhoven, and Peter, responsible for the new packaging plant Bordpak, played with Ewert Brice. Ewert would not mind me saying he was half the size of Peter. This particular evening they were returning from French lessons at the French Embassy. Peter opened the bidding and Ewert replied in French. I will never forget Peter saying 'Ewert I can never understand your bidding in English how do you expect me to understand in French.' Great times to remember.

I had been offered other opportunities within the company but remained with BEAM for over ten years. There is a great satisfaction in reflecting on how many Nigerians took responsibility for the success we achieved. I had great faith in them and feel this was reciprocated.

Chapter 5 – Vono Products Ltd

One day in late 1975, I had a call from the UAC Chairman in Nigeria, Fred Pardoe. He said "Alan, we would like you to take over as the Managing Director of Vono Products Ltd." The factory and offices were in Mushin on the mainland. After a pause, I said yes, provided I can remain in our present house. He agreed and I duly handed BEAM over to Felix Osifo. We were given a tremendous send-off by the staff. On one occasion they had taken over the Cathy Chinese restaurant and we were fortunate to have all the children with us. Football matches and so many personal gifts that we have treasured over the years. So to a completely different business. Vono Products Ltd had been a joint venture between Duport Ltd and UAC to manufacture metal bed frames, small folding beds and later interior sprung mattresses. The Nigerian Enterprises Promotion Decree1977 provides for sixty percent of the shareholding to be in Nigerian hands.

VONO AGM
The young man seated in a white coat was destined to become the
Interim President August 1993

Vono Board Meeting – Three very capable Nigerian Directors

The company was situated on the mainland in Mushin. With the traffic congestion, I would leave Ikoyi no later than 7 am. I still had my driver James. The factory occupied a large area with a spacious metal factory, smaller mattress production area, storage, and offices. The previous Managing Director, undoubtedly destined for bigger things, was sadly killed in a road accident. However, the business seemed to have no clear direction for its future. Stocks of obsolete items were very high and we were still carrying out time and motion studies on things such as the small beds when in other parts of the country local people were making them at much lower prices. Within the business, there were very good Nigerians with university backgrounds. Three were Board members covering Secretary/Commercial, Marketing and an assistant to the Factory Manager who was the only other expatriate. All made a significant contribution once we were able to plan for the future.

The business had to find a new direction and whilst we were the only company with the capability of producing an interior sprung mattress we did not make a complete bed. It seemed that there was a growing part of the population who would welcome the availability of a complete bed with an interior sprung mattress as opposed to a foam mattress. In simplistic terms, this was the change in the fortunes of the company over the next two years.

Much had to be done. One thing that would greatly improve the lives of the workforce was improving the meal served at lunchtime. To this end, we added a further floor to the office building enabling improvements to both cooking facilities and seating. I remember well the smart and efficient lady who was responsible for all aspects of catering. I shared a room with my colleagues and had lunch at the factory regularly.

There had to be a radical reduction in the areas of obsolete stock and the volume of metal products we manufactured in the future. Most important was our ability to offer a complete bed. Our main problem would be size and logistics. Dealers throughout the country had relatively small premises and storage of these large packages could be difficult. For the complete bed, we needed ends to support our metal base frame. I turned to my friends at Harmony House who was a short distance away and they gladly designed attractive wooden ends, and that left us with packaging. Here we were able to obtain the service of Bordpak in making a large carton to house the complete bed. Then came distribution and we invested in two vehicles with trailers capable of holding 50 beds. With the advertising skills of Lintas, we launched SLEEPWELL – your perfect sleeping partner. It was an exciting programme and the large vehicles moving throughout the country made an excellent advertising platform.

Lorries for distribution of the complete bed

No doubt there were a number of difficult times but the only one that comes to mind was the day a tanker delivered our fuel supplies. As he left the factory his vehicle struck the pipe leading to our fuel tank and very quickly inflammable liquid was spreading as there was a slight gradient. All members of the staff recognised the seriousness of the situation and acted accordingly. I think we were about three days before normality returned. In two years the business moved forward both in profitability and capital employed. Shortly after being appointed Managing Director, I was asked to become Chairman. It would be less than honest to say that literally facing hundreds of shareholders I would not be nervous. I quickly realised that being involved in the daily running of the business made answering questions that much easier.

I said I would return to the subject of golf in reference to the Ikoyi club. I was a member but a game in which I never made a great deal of progress. Popular with the military and a few Nigerians who with limited opportunities had excelled in the game. Over a number of years, during the European winter, most of the leading names would compete in an African tour. Nick Faldo, Tony Jacklin for example would be flown to Nigeria, then Ghana, then to East Africa by Caledonian Airways, free of charge. They would be accommodated and entertained by various residents. We were delighted to have Tommy Horton stay with us the year after he won the four-day competition. In my former days, we provided a Burrows punch card machine and there is Lee Elder, the American winner that year, trying to get to grips with the machine. The money must have meant a great deal in those days when foreign exchange could be remitted, but what a different world golf is today.

At Vono, I was anxious to encourage these few very talented Nigerian players, feeling that they suffered from not having a regular competition environment. I approached the golf club captain to see if the club would allow this limited number of players to have a competition amongst themselves. It would take place during the monthly mug for members and we would give a sum of money to the top three. I am pleased to say the club agreed and the Nigerians would tee off ahead of members. It was pleasing to see one of these Nigerians, runner up to a visiting professional.

It must have been April, May 1977 I was in the office at the usual time and there was a knock on the door and my secretary announced that Mr Abebe and a guest wished to see me. At that time Chris was the Chairman of UAC Nigeria and with him the Chairman of UAC UK, Frazer Sedcole. Chris was the first Nigerian Chairman with many years of experience in personnel. Very approachable and pleased to say his life span was over one hundred years. We had a long discussion about the business and then a tour of the factory. I cannot recall any difficult moments except the surprise of seeing them so early in the morning. Daphne and I were invited to a reception for Frazer at the Metropolitan Club that evening and at some stage in proceedings, Frazer came over to me and in a conversation that probably lasted twenty minutes, asked if I would be prepared to return to the UK. A new Building Materials Division was being established of which I would be a board member.

UAC already had Kennedys, a builder's merchant and garden centre with HQ in Bournemouth and of course, there were the overseas companies in the same activity. I think my first reaction was the opportunity to see more of the children before they had flown the nest. Suffice it to say my answer was in the affirmative. There was all the packing after so many years and the farewells given to us by staff were incredible considering the relatively short time I had been with Vono. Once again I had received outstanding support from the Africans within the business and none more so than my secretary who I mentioned above.

She would have been an asset to any international company. Before leaving Daphne and I visited most of our main dealers in the country. I think we left Nigeria sometime in August but I had to make a special trip back in late September to chair my second Vono shareholders' meeting.

When we left in August, Stephen was with us and would return to school for his last term before university. Our planned journey was to fly along the coast as we wished to see Anne and Arthur Draper before we flew to Lisbon and then America to see my sister and family. Stephen would fly back to the UK. We stayed with Anne and Arthur for seven relaxing and enjoyable days. Such a wonderful experience to be back where our lives started together.

Chapter 6 – We return to the UK

I am going to digress at this stage as I would like to say a few more words about the Gambia. I have spoken extensively on the camaraderie that existed amongst those who had worked together in the 1950s. When back in the UK, Ken Gibson who was the person to advise me I was a father. Ken organized reunions over two nights at various locations and was very well attended.

1990 marked the twenty-five years of The Gambia Independence. David Niven received a letter from Harry Lloyd Evans whose father had been commissioner of police in the 1950s. The letter invited us all to join them for their independence celebrations. Flights and hotels were booked and what a memorable visit we all had. You will recall when we were there the economy was almost completely dependent upon groundnuts. Now the accent was as a winter holiday destination with good hotels built along the Atlantic coastline. We all flew out together and days were busy catching up on all the simple, but new experiences that now existed. Unfortunately Banjul formally Bathurst, whilst old when we were there, appeared neglected. With fond memories of a visit to the church where we were married. As did Emily and

Charles Myers. There was the day we were in two long canoes, bird watching. We had our breakfast in a thatched hut on the water's edge and the descent to the canoes proved an obstacle course in itself and reminded us the years had passed by. One of the most memorable trips was up to James Island. The river was well known to most of us but an English couple had a powered boat in which they could accommodate large groups of visitors. On a beautiful day, we left Banjul and our first stop was Albreda. As we approached the jetty, sitting on a low wall were twenty or so small children. They all knew that if they behaved themselves the lady of the boat, who was very strict, would give them each a sweet. What a simple but endearing sight. Enjoying a good lunch and then to James Island, an infamous location with its history of the slave trade. We had passed many times but never visited. Its past disgrace to humanity is something we had not been prepared to face. On the return journey, we had Dolphins enjoying themselves. Our approach to Banjul was disappointing as we could see the wreckage of both Lady Wright and Fuladu.

Then to the big day. A very large stadium newly built at Ikeja overflowing with those wishing to be present at what would be a historic day. This very small country, for so long being part of the British empire. Harry Lloyd Evans was there to show us to our seats which were almost directly behind the representatives of different countries. Princess Anne, George Bush junior. I think this was only the second time he had been out of America.

Firstly the military bands were followed by probably six platoons of smart and efficient soldiers.

Finally, President Jawarra arrived accompanied by the Nigerian head of state General Babangida. One witnessed an occasion that would have been a credit to any nation. Afterwards, we were able to relax in the company of Mr and Mrs Lloyd Evans and their friends. I recall at the hotel that evening was a group of Nigerian dancers. Firstly they tempted David Niven onto the stage, then Daphne, and she did not disgrace herself.

President Jawarra our veterinary surgeon, was a friend of Arthur Draper then Chairman of the Gambia Marketing Board. They shared an interest in golf. Arthur designed and put in place a golf course in Fajara. I believe there might have also been one hole in the grounds of the government house.

We were able to have a meal with Peter N'Dow and Daphne made contact with Julie Williams. David, Ken, Daphne, and I also made time to visit Sanjali Bojang who was very disappointed that so few of us attended an elaborate party he had arranged with native dancers and drummers. Not sure of the details but being a popular man he at some stage had clashed with authorities and he seemed to be quite proud of the bullet holes in the walls of his house. Still a delightful man who I am proud to have known.

Jallow and Sanjali
The two Headmen who gave me total loyalty and advice

I am sure returning to the UK was a real culture shock. During those latter years in Africa, there had been a number of people at hand to assist. Whether rain or mainly sunshine there always seemed to be a freshness about each day. In the UK getting things done seemed to involve such lengthy discussion with inevitable delay.

Although the initial briefing I received was straightforward, as things finally emerged I was back in an environment that suited me. UAC had already acquired Builders Merchants with garden centres with their headquarters in Bournemouth. Peter Tueart, having returned to Bournemouth some years earlier, was the general manager of this business. Informing a Division the intention was to bring together the UK and overseas interests. I remember well my first meeting with Peter in Bournemouth and his first words, "Am I going to be your boss, or are you going to be mine?" At that stage, Peter obviously was not aware he was destined for a place on the mainboard in London. However, although Frazer Sedcole had advised me that I would be responsible for the whole division, after a period of indecision it was announced that I would have responsibility for the overseas interests, and a colleague I knew well would be responsible for the UK. In retrospect, this was a blessing as in so many ways it gave me the freedom of action I had always enjoyed.

There followed a six-month period in which I would need to be with G B Ollivant in Manchester as they were responsible for the part of the business I would inherit. There were two questions to be answered, namely, the staff required and where we should be based. We spent what would have been six very pleasant months acclimatising ourselves to this new environment apart from one major incident in our lives. The company rented a delightful house in Adlington and with a short walk to the station, I could commute into Manchester. Fine for this short period, but not sure this could have been a lifetime experience. The incident I refer to is, Daphne had been shopping with Dulcie Wolff in Manchester. I was at lunch when a call came from Jim Louden's secretary to say his car was coming to take me to Royal Salfords hospital. Daphne had collapsed in Manchester. I arrived to find Daphne awake and smiling but the medical team was not sure what the problem might be. Then they decided she should go through the scanning machine only to discover a large growth in the front of her brain. A leading surgeon from New Zealand decided he would operate immediately. It was so fortunate that the ambulance was from Salfords hospital as at that time it was the only scanning machine in the NW of England, and very early days for this type of operation. I could not begin to describe the night I had and when I went into the hospital the next day, Daphne was completely frozen. A few days later those smiles had returned and once again we had so much to be thankful for. It was not long before we had leased the ground floor of a new development in Bournemouth and selected those members of staff who would transfer south. In a very quick time, we were a small team who gave me tremendous support.

The Gottschalck business was now entirely building materials, no longer involved with textiles or office equipment. It was sixteen years since I left Aba and on my first visit, I felt the business had not changed over those years. However, Nigeria had changed with local manufacture in a number of areas all of which were available to contractors and traders.

In very few areas had there been a realistic attempt to add value in the form of service. An exception to this was Braithwaite tanks where we had always received such support from that company. There was an approach to sell and subsequently manufacture a network of metal frames that would cover large roofed areas. A fabrication plant was established which I hoped would subsequently enable us to manufacture a wind pump and other metal requirements for Braithwaite. I formed a very close relationship with Intermediate Technology Development Techniques Ltd who had already established a manufacturing unit in Kenya. More of that later. The main task was to rationalize the existing

Gottschalck business and move into more specialized areas. For a period of seven years, I must have spent at least eight weeks actually in Nigeria. Oil continued to see significant changes in the country and many not to the benefit of the majority of the population.

Early wind pump manufacture in East Africa

I looked at the middle east and at that stage, we did not have any product or service that was not already well established in that region. Then we had a request from a Saudi family wanting to establish a builders' merchants. I visited the country and this resulted in us seconding a member of staff for a set period and our receiving a significant order with cash in advance. From an early stage it was apparent this would not be a lasting relationship. However due to the volume of such products as sealants we had purchased for the overseas business we were in a position to own a brand under Kennedy's label. Although one tried to rationalize and move Gottschalck in a different direction this would take time and prompted me to explore in-depth the creation of a water resources business. I felt no company was better placed than UAC to provide this vital service. Irrespective of what the future might hold this would always be a flagship for the company and at an early stage, it had the backing of the mainboard. It would be a business with the capability of locating, extracting, storing, and distributing this precious commodity.

Early 1980 UAC Project
To form a Water Resources Unit

To assist in this project Brian Walker from Unilever Organization Division joined me and became not only a colleague equally committed to the project but a good friend. Projects would be in the name of and managed by UAC. However individual parts of a project would involve technical partners. Mander, Raikes and Marshall civil engineering consultants with a wide experience in hydro-geology in

Africa and the Middle East had agreed to join a consortium. This would include George Stow Ltd. Specializing in drilling and water engineering. They have operated for many years in West Africa and we have worked with their associate company on a number of occasions. Braithwaite Ltd would complete the Water Resources Group. We appreciated from the outset that a vital aspect would be the funding of projects.

To this end Unilever, public relations arranged a series of meetings and presentations by Brian and myself. These included the world bank in America together with a number of large charities mainly in New York. Then to the European centre for agriculture in Rome, Trade-in Vienna with Brian going to Brussels. Without exception, when it was known that Unilever represented by UAC would be involved there was enthusiastic support. I had prepared a feasibility study in November 1984 and when all strands of the project were complete Brian was able to prepare a very detailed study in early 1985.

This was accompanied by initial advertising material. I am not a party to the exact timing but it was not long after this stage had been reached, the Unilever board felt UAC would cease to play a part in its longer-term plans. End of water and the beginning of many changes to the company in which I had experienced such a challenging and enjoyable thirty-four years. I was due to retire at the end of 1985 and the intervening period of uncertainty within UAC demonstrated to me the problems so many younger generations might face.

Although finalizing the affairs of such a large and diverse organization would take a number of years, certain things could be actioned quickly and the relatively newly formed Building Materials division was an early casualty. All staff was assisted in various ways and we all had the satisfaction of knowing the unit in Bournemouth had contributed to the centre in every year of its existence. I was asked to come to London as a divisional commercial director. The main thing I remember about this relatively short period was the daily commute to London, with time to read.

Chapter 7 – Uganda

It was July and the last six months with the company. If I had known exactly what the situation was I might well have refused to go. The communication went something like this. The expatriate currently Chairman of Gailey and Roberts Uganda is leaving and we feel the business at that time, solely Caterpillar earth moving equipment is ready for expansion into other product areas. We would like you to go for six months with the objective of recommending potential areas for expansion. You will recall we had an experience of the country whilst stationed in Nigeria and Winston Churchill referred to it as the pearl of Africa. Regardless of what would face Daphne and me, I can appreciate this statement.

I had never been faced with such a misleading message on the part of the company. However, regardless of how things would unfold, I am pleased we went as it gave me yet another perspective of Africa.

We flew with British Airways to Nairobi. In discussions with the general manager of our associate company in Kenya, it was obvious that the situation in Kampala was not one that Daphne should be exposed to. Our elder son and family were at that time in Malawi and arrangements were made for her to fly to Blantyre for a stay that proved to be far longer than expected.

I then flew to Kampala to be met by the person leaving the company and taken to what had been a most attractive residence but now resembled fort Knox with iron grills in all directions. There was a rather bedraggled military presence with occasional gunfire during the day which became fairly continuous at night. Handover such as it was completed and shortly I was on my own. The business was rather like the country, run down.

Our house in Kampala
Inside likened to Fort Knox

At one stage all items within the house were new and worked. Now very few things were fit for purpose. Remember the Gambia thirty-five years ago. Then all was basic but you had the means of making it function effectively. It was difficult to fully appreciate what had happened in those intervening years. However, it did not take me long to realize that I had around me an excellent team of Ugandan staff. The missing elements had been purpose and leadership. I quickly made contact with the British high commission who were excellent throughout the difficult times ahead. Events moved forward at pace and I may not be quite correct in how I record them. There was one young expatriate engineer on the team. I suppose it was some two weeks after I had taken over that I realized the commercial manager Bill Kigosi was accepted as an obvious leader of the team and would give me flexibility in the difficult weeks ahead.

Early one morning there was continuous gunfire which was the child army from the commercial south lead by the now President Museveni, entering Kampala. They had been training in forest areas and were to defeat the government supported by the military personnel from the north of Uganda. I may have commented before on the fact that under British rule we seemed to have concentrated on peoples from northern areas when establishing a military presence. In this respect, Museveni seemed to be an exception. Under these circumstances, I felt, with the business closed the young expatriate and I should move to Nairobi. Not an easy journey by road but we made it and I was in daily telephone contact with Bill Kigosi. This break lasted a matter of weeks during which time I flew to Entebbe on two occasions. One I remember well as we lost one of the two engines of the aircraft. However, the pilot made a very good landing. During each of these visits, I became increasingly impressed with this disciplined young army.

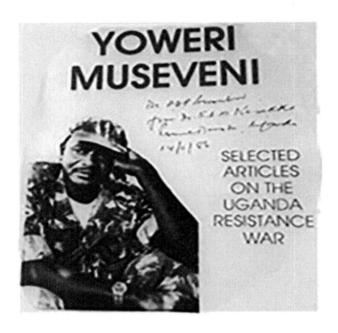

Yoweri Museveni 1986

Although short of uniforms, when stopped they were polite in their dealings and my experience never looked for a reward. Being able to touch base with Bill made a real contribution to establishing our priorities for the future.

The period in Kenya enabled me to make contact with Bob Harries who had developed the Kijito windpump in conjunction with Intermediate Technology. Bob was an interesting man whose family had been in Thika for many years, mainly involved with agriculture. He was a pilot in his own right and subsequently flew to Uganda when we knew the government was interested in the wind pump.

Back to Uganda and time to execute plans for the future. During the remaining time spent in Uganda, there was unease as the new government established itself.

Gailey and Roberts did not have sufficient funds to meet monthly expenses. The only asset we did have was land. We divided the large company site. Constructed new offices and other facilities within our existing stores/workshop. With this complete, we had no difficulty in renting the now-vacant site and able to generate a monthly surplus.

Looking back through the papers I still have of this period, I am surprised how many handwritten reports and schedules there are, indicating the shortage of typing facilities.

Rather like those early days in Kaur.

I mentioned the very pleasant bungalow and the security precautions that had been taken. Behind the large verandah was an original folding metal screen, behind this was metal bar doors. A further grill door took you to a corridor on the right was a kitchen and left bedrooms. Both had grill doors. Likewise, all windows had the same type of security. It was a bungalow and I remember looking up from my bed at a Celotex ceiling. All that remained was a simple tile roof. A fairly easy way to make an entry.

Daphne had been staying with family in Malawi and I think it was about six weeks before we were due to return to the UK. I flew to Blantyre and we returned to Kampala. As usual, she accepted conditions as they were and like myself looks back on this period with much affection. We had two members of staff. Connie cooked and helped in the house. She had a very difficult life after losing her husband but was a mature and very intelligent lady. With Daphne's movements becoming somewhat restricted it would not be exaggerating to say they became friends. Daphne enjoyed spending time with her in the kitchen and helping with the preparation of different dishes to those we might normally expect. There was also a common interest in sewing. By contrast in the garden was Kamisi. A tall, jovial young man with relatives from north Africa. Again Daphne enjoyed his company and nothing was too much trouble. We had a problem with the water supply which stemmed from the tank on the roof. I probably should not continue with this incident but I climbed onto the roof with Kamisi who quickly identified a faulty part. Without a word, off he went only to return in about thirty minutes with a replacement part. I never questioned him but have a feeling that there would be another household in Kampala having trouble with their water supply that night.

Kamisi and I
Try to repair a water problem

Two people expecting very little, but a joy to be with.

The staff and so many people we had met in our very short time in Uganda gave us a tremendous farewell. Kamisi had grown a flower in a 60w light bulb for Daphne and I had a pair of perfectly usable drinking glasses made from beer bottles.

The letters of appreciation from Bill Kigosi and others we will always treasure.

Bill Kigozi and his wife
Amongst many capable Uganda people we were privileged to meet